Developing a Spiritual Foundation

Christian discipleship for the Deaf

Student Edition

Copyright © 2015, Converge Great Lakes. All rights reserved. Adapted from materials provided by Gary Rohrmayer, Your Journey Resources (www.yourjourney.org). Used by permission.

Cover design by Hans Clough (HansClough.com) and Dwight Clough (DwightClough.com). Image adapted from a photo by Jesus Rodriguez, Flickr, Creative Commons License.

Developing a Spiritual Foundation

Welcome to an Adventure of a Lifetime

At the end of the Walt Disney movie, *Hook*, Robin Williams (who played Peter Pan's role) said, "Life—that's the biggest adventure." As a Christian, we know that following Jesus is the biggest adventure of all. If we travel through life the way God intended and designed, we will find complete satisfaction and fulfillment. This book/class is designed to help you experience an exciting adventure of living with Jesus Christ. It does not matter if you are a new believer or have been a Christian for many years. This adventure of following Jesus as your Lord will allow you to enjoy the blessings of God's kingdom. It will also prepare you to help share the gospel with other people around you.

To receive the greatest benefit from these lessons, you should answer the questions quickly and honestly. You do not have to worry about your answers, or try to think too deeply to find the correct answers. It is best to write down your feelings and beliefs. As you study together in class, your leader will help show you the truth about yourself and God's Word. Then you will become all that God wants you to be, a true follower of Jesus Christ.

So, on to the journey we go!

(Adapted from the words of Gary Rohmayer.)

Table of Contents

	Reviewing your spiritual journey	4
#1	My New Security in Christ: How you know you are a true Christian	14
#2	My New Life in Christ: How to grow in my new faith	26
#3	My New Commitment: Baptism: Who should be baptized? When should you be baptized and why?	37
#4	My New Family in Christ: Get involved with the church	48
#5	My New Freedom in Christ: How to experience God's forgiveness	60
#6	My New Road Map for Life: Understanding the Bible	73
#7	My New Ambition for Life: How to honor Jesus with my lifestyle	86
#8	My New Power for Living: How to "tune in" to the Holy Spirit	98
#9	My New Choice in Christ: Defeating temptation in your life	110
#10	My New Privilege: Sharing my faith/witnessing effectively	122
	Where Do We Go From Here?	134
	About Converge Great Lakes Deaf Ministries	142

Reviewing Your Spiritual Journey

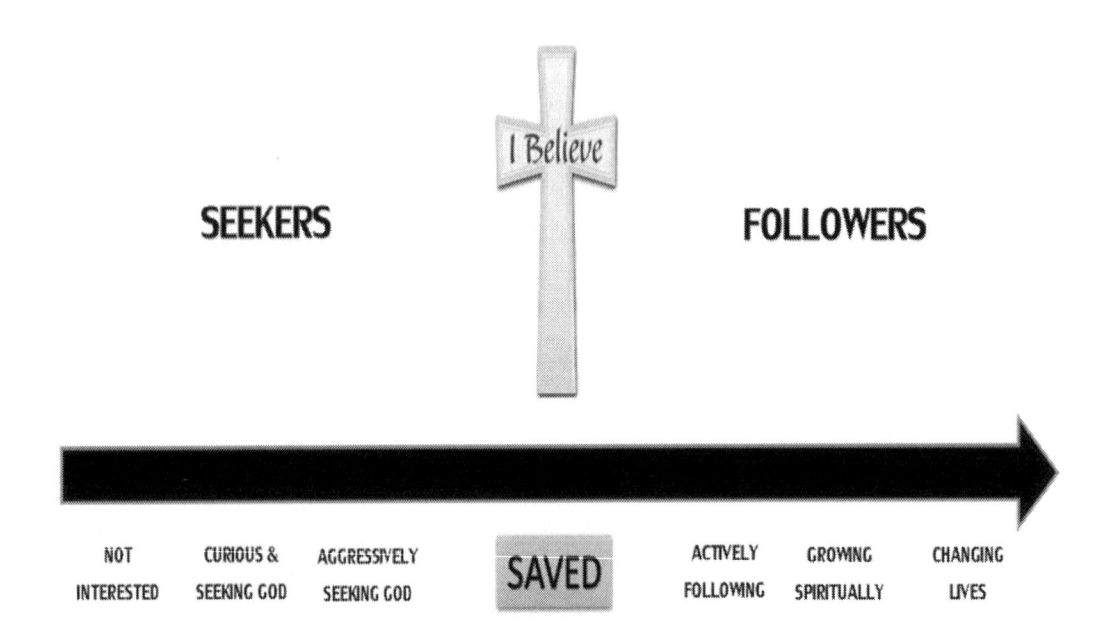

SEEKERS — I Believe — **FOLLOWERS**

NOT INTERESTED | CURIOUS & SEEKING GOD | AGGRESSIVELY SEEKING GOD | SAVED | ACTIVELY FOLLOWING | GROWING SPIRITUALLY | CHANGING LIVES

1. Explain in your own words, what is the difference between seekers and followers:

(a) A seeker of spiritual issues is what?

(b) A follower of Christ is what?

2. How long have you been a Christian as a follower of Christ? (Put a check mark by your experience—how long you are a Christian or a follower of Christ.)

_____ Less than 6 months

_____ Less than 1 year

_____ Less than 2 years

_____ Less than 5 years

Other: _____

3. What is your past experience with Christianity? (Put a check mark by your experience.)

_____ No experience. I never went to church.

_____ No experience. I never read the Bible.

_____ I went to church as a child.

_____ I go to church but I do not understand it.

_____ I do not feel comfortable in a church.

_____ I am not interested in church or Bible.

_____ I am a Christian, but I am not active follower of Christ.

_____ I am a Christian and an active follower of Christ.

4. Who in your family are Christian and are truly followers of Jesus?

_____ My mother

_____ My father

_____ My brother

_____ My sister

_____ None of them

_____ I am the first Christian in my family.

_____ Other relatives that are Christians

_____ I don't know.

5. Explain how you chose faith in Jesus Christ?

_____ A family member encouraged/influenced me.

_____ A friend encouraged/influenced me.

_____ A person I respect encouraged/influenced me.

_____ A pastor encouraged/influenced me.

_____ A Christian TV show influenced me.

_____ Other:

6. Explain the day when you became saved (Christian). How did it happen? Tell us your story of how you were saved.

7. Explain about your parents' Christian life. (Put a check mark by your experience.)

_____ They are actively involved following Christ.

_____ They go to church every Sunday.

_____ They don't talk about their beliefs.

_____ They do not go to church often.

_____ They are not Christians.

_____ Other (explain below):

_____

_____

_____

8. What religion or religious groups did you follow in the past?

_____

_____

_____

9. Write down (in short) **about your past religious experiences or supernatural experiences** (seems humanly impossible situation/event that happened).

_____

_____

_____

_____

10. List the names of 3 people that influenced your life in a spiritual way (told you positive things about God).

1. _____

2. _____

3. _____

11. Explain what kind of person you are. (Put a check mark by your experience.)

_____ I am thankful for my past life and I feel satisfied.

_____ I would like to change my past life.

_____ I believe life is valuable. I am trying to live the best I can.

_____ I like other people.

_____ I relate well, (get along good), with my family and friends.

_____ I can make close relationships with people easy. I give and receive love.

_____ I do not feel important to others.

_____ I do not feel loved by other people.

_____ I am a very open person. I am not afraid to let other people know me.

_____ I am afraid to let people know about my private life.

_____ I am a very private person. I don't want people to know me deeply.

_____ I don't like to give or help other people. I enjoy receiving things from them.

_____ I never had someone explain the Bible to me.

_____ I want to learn more about the Bible and I am ready for someone to teach me.

_____ I want to learn how to share my faith with my family and friends.

_____ I want to help people become a Christian and know Jesus as Savior and Lord.

12. What things help you learn?

_____ I read a lot. Books help me learn most.

_____ I am not a good reader and do not learn much from books.

_____ I learn better if I watch someone and then copy them (get involved and help).

_____ I find people who can help me learn. They know what I want to know.

_____ I learn from visual examples/illustrations. (Pictures, videos, drawings, etc.)

_____ It is hard for me to learn.

13. How do you make decisions?

_____ I am quick to do things before I think about it.

_____ I do whatever feels right.

_____ I ask close friends or people I respect to help me decide what to do.

_____ I obey rules/laws/principles. (I act according to rules.)

_____ I ask God to guide me and show me.

_____ I watch other people and judge their decisions (if it was good or bad decision).

_____ I do not have a special way to make decisions.

14. I want to finish this book/class in…

(Put a check mark to show when you want to finish the class.)

_____ 3 months

_____ 6 months

_____ 9 months

_____ 1 year

Developing a Spiritual Foundation

Lesson #1

My New Security in Christ

What does "Christian" mean?

_____

_____

_____

_____

_____

Christian Life Quiz

(Evaluate your beliefs before we begin Lesson #1.)

1. How can you become a Christian? (Put "x" in front of correct answer.)

_____ If you live a good life, you are a Christian.

_____ If you go to church and pray, you are a Christian.

_____ If you obey God's commandments and live with good behavior. For example: do not get drunk, no drugs, no sex if not married, no adultery (means no sex with other people, only your spouse), etc.

_____ You believe and have faith in the Lord Jesus death on cross paid for your sins, and His death and blood is the only way you can go to heaven.

_____ Because you saw a "supernatural event" (an impossible situation happen). (For example: you think you saw an angel, or bright light, or something happened that is not normal and you cannot explain it.)

_____ Not sure. (I don't know.)

2. How you can know you are a true Christian? Everyone has problems and some times you doubt God loves you and wants to work in your life. Put an "x" by the sentence you think describes what a Christian is.

_____ That person does not have problems in life.

_____ That person goes to church a lot and prays.

_____ That person feels they are a Christian.

_____ That person believes and trusts that Jesus death on cross paid for their sins, and Jesus death and blood is the only reason they can go to heaven.

_____ They are Christian because they experienced a "supernatural" event (example: saw a bright light or something they cannot explain that made them feel good).

_____ Not sure.

Developing a Spiritual Foundation

3. Do you think or believe that God does not want to be involved in your life? Why?

_____

_____

_____

_____

_____

Lesson #1: My New Security in Christ: How you know you are a true Christian

1. Read the Bible passages and answer the questions.

To become 100% sure that you are a Christian, then you must realize that Jesus' death on cross was more than enough to cancel your punishment. His death gives you the right (like a ticket) to enter heaven.

a. Who did Jesus die for? Does that include you? (John 3:16, 1 Timothy 2:6)

_____

_____

b. Christ's death on cross was called a… (Hebrews 9:26-28)

c. Christ's death on cross was called a… (Romans 8:3)

d. Christ's death on cross was called a… (Mark 10:45)

e. What does all of this make you feel?

f. Why did Christ die for us? (1 Peter 3:18)

Developing a Spiritual Foundation

g. What did Jesus say on the cross (the last 3 words He spoke)? (John 19:30)

_____

_____

h. What did God say you will have? (1 John 5:13)

_____

i. What must you do before you can experience this promise? (1 John 5:12)

_____

_____

j. What happens if you do not have faith and are not connected to Jesus?
Read 1 John 5:12, John 3:36.

_____

_____

_____

Developing a Spiritual Foundation

2. Read the Bible passages below and answer the questions.

If you want to be a 100% confident believer, you must understand that God's promise of eternal life is only because of His mercy. You do not receive eternal life because you are a good person and do good things. It is not your works that save you. God saves us only because of His grace and mercy. We cannot work to earn our salvation by doing good things.

a. God saves you because of His... (Titus 3:5, Ephesians 2:8)

_____

b. You can't do what? (Ephesians 2:9)

_____

_____

3. God wants us to be 100% followers of Jesus. God will work in our lives in three ways. What are those three ways?

a. Through the... (Romans 10:17, 1 John 5:13)

_____

Developing a Spiritual Foundation

b. Through His… (Romans 8:16)

_____

c. He will… (2 Corinthians 5:17)

_____

God's Word will never change. In Matthew 24:35, Jesus says, "Heaven and earth will fade away, but my words will never fade away." Sometimes during our life, our feelings can make us doubt/not believe God's Word. But our faith is based on God's truths, not on our feelings or situations. On the next page is a chart to help you understand how important it is for us to focus on facts/truths in God's Word; and not on our feelings or situations.

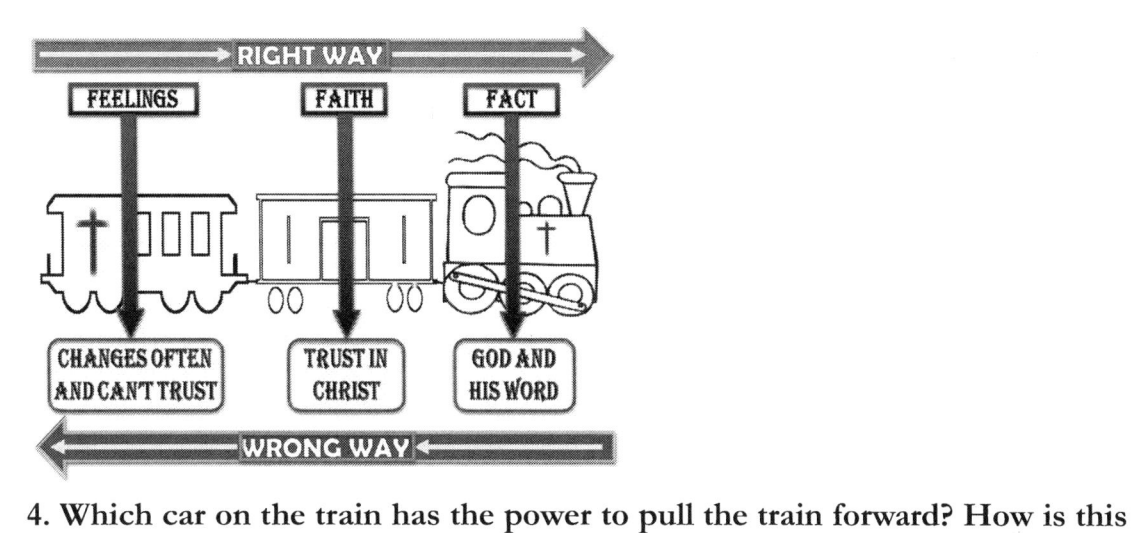

Developing a Spiritual Foundation

```
         → RIGHT WAY →
  FEELINGS   FAITH    FACT
     ↓        ↓        ↓
  CHANGES   TRUST    GOD AND
  OFTEN AND   IN     HIS WORD
  CAN'T TRUST CHRIST
         ← WRONG WAY ←
```

4. Which car on the train has the power to pull the train forward? How is this example of the train the same as the Christian life?

_____

_____

_____

5. We should believe 100% that God's Word is truth/fact. How does the Bible explain people who do not use faith and allow their feelings to control them? Read James 1:6 and then explain:

_____

_____

_____

Developing a Spiritual Foundation

6. To live your new life in Christ, you must understand what happened to you when you were saved and trusted Jesus Christ as your Lord and Savior. Look below; there is a list of truths that happened to you spiritually when you were saved. Explain each on the lines below.

a. John 1:12

b. Ephesians 1:13-14

c. Ephesians 2:5

d. Romans 5:1

e. Revelation 3:5, 20:12, 20:15, 21:27

f. Colossians 1:14

_____

g. Which one of these recent verses (above) are the most important to you right now?

_____

_____

7. Finish these sentences below and discuss them in class.

In this lesson, I learned

_____

_____

_____

_____

Developing a Spiritual Foundation

This lesson helped me believe

_____

_____

_____

I feel

_____

_____

_____

Weekly Assignments

1. Begin reading the Gospel (book in New Testament) of Mark.

2. Write out and memorize (remember deep in your mind) this verse: 1 John 5:13

_____

_____

_____

_____

_____

3. Pick one thing you learned from this lesson and tell/share with a family member or friend.

Developing a SPIRITUAL Foundation

Lesson #2

My New Life in Christ

How to grow in my new faith

Christian Life Quiz

(Evaluate your opinion of spiritual growth before we begin Lesson #2.)

What does it mean to grow in your Christian life?

You choose in order of importance: (#1 = very, very important), (#2 = very important, (#3 = important), (#4 = little important), (#5 = not important), (#6 = don't care).

____ be active in church.

____ do devotions/read Bible every day.

____ share with others about Jesus.

____ serve/help in church.

____ go to church and worship every week.

____ learn deeper truths in the Bible.

____ learn how to open my heart and share/give my money.

Lesson #2: My New Life in Christ: How to grow in my new faith

1. We need to feel secure about our relationship with Christ. In 2 Peter 3:17-18, it says we grow in the

_____

and

_____

of our Lord and Savior Jesus Christ.

2. Write down your thoughts and/or ideas how you can grow in knowledge and understand more about the grace that Jesus gives you.

a. To learn more knowledge of Christ, I can (I can do what?)

_____

_____

b. To learn more about the grace that Jesus gives us, I can (I can do what?)

_____

_____

Developing a Spiritual Foundation

3. There are three things you can do step by step to grow in your faith in our Lord Jesus Christ.

a. Read Acts 2:42 and find 3 ways to grow in Jesus Christ.

1. _____

2. _____

3. _____

b. Which one is easiest for you? Why?

_____

_____

4. I can grow in Christ through prayer.

a. Why is prayer important? Read the verses and write your answers.

Proverbs 15:8

_____

_____

Developing a Spiritual Foundation

John 16:24

Matthew 26:41

Philippians 4:6,7

b. Write down a list of things that cause you to stop praying. What blocks your prayers to God?

1 Peter 3:7

Psalm 66:18

Developing a Spiritual Foundation

James 4:3

Hebrews 11:6

Is there anything in this list that is blocking your prayers today?

c. How can you pray deeply with power?

James 5:16

1 Thessalonians 5:16-18

Matthew 7:7-11

_____

_____

d. Prayer is (choose one or more):

_____ Easy for me

_____ Difficult for me

_____ Not normal to me

_____ Gives me peace

e. Write down a list from your mind of a few ways you can improve/grow in your personal (private) prayer life:

_____

_____

_____

5. I can grow in Christ by studying God's Word (the Bible).

a. Studying the Bible will give me (what?)

Psalm 119:165

John 8:32

Psalm 119:105

b. How can I understand my Bible better?

   1. RETREAT (go) to a quiet place.

   2. RELY (depend) on the Holy Spirit to teach me.

   3. READ continuously until I feel God speak to me.

   4. REFLECT on (think deeply about) what I read.

   5. RESPOND to (do) what God said to me in the Bible verses.

   6. REALIGN (change and line-up) my life to match God's Word.

   7. REST (believe and have peace) in God's promises.

Something to think about: "A Bible that is old and falling apart usually belongs to someone who is not falling apart."

6. I can grow in Christ when I am with God's people (other believers).

a. Read Acts 2:42-47. These verses explain that in the beginning of the church, Christians were strongly united with each other. Write down a list of ways how they helped each other out.

_____

_____

_____

_____

Developing a Spiritual Foundation

b. Write down ideas how our "fellowship time together" can help us/benefit us.

_____

_____

_____

_____

c. What are the benefits of serving Christ and helping others in the church?
(What can we get out of it?)

John 12:26

_____

John 13:35

_____

_____

Write down a list of ways you can begin serving in church.

_____

_____

_____

7. Finish these sentences below and discuss them in class.

In this lesson, I learned

_____

_____

_____

_____

This lesson helped me believe

_____

_____

_____

I feel

_____

_____

_____

Developing a Spiritual Foundation

Weekly Assignments

1. Continue reading the book of Mark in the New Testament.

2. Find your skills, talents and abilities. Use them to help your church right now.

3. Write out and memorize (remember deep in your mind) this verse: (2 Peter 3:18)

_____

_____

_____

_____

4. Pick one thing you learned from this lesson and tell/share with a family member or friend.

Lesson #3

My New Commitment

Baptism: Who should be baptized? When should you be baptized and why?

Christian Life Quiz

(Evaluate your beliefs before we begin Lesson #3.)

1. What do you believe about baptism?

____ If I die and was never baptized, I will be in "limbo" (space between heaven and hell).

____ If I am not baptized, then I will go to hell when I die.

____ If I am not baptized, then I cannot participate in communion at church.

____ If I am not baptized, then I will not receive the Holy Spirit.

____ If I am not baptized, then my sins will not be forgiven.

Developing a Spiritual Foundation

2. Why should you be baptized?

____ I should be baptized so my sins can be forgiven.

____ I should be baptized so I can join a church.

____ I should be baptized so I can go to heaven.

____ I should be baptized so I can show my personal faith in Jesus Christ.

____ I don't know why I should be baptized.

Lesson #3: My New Commitment: Baptism: Who should be baptized? When should you be baptized and why?

1. The New Testament explains the reason for baptism. What do these verses say you should <u>do</u> before you are baptized? <u>Who</u> should be baptized? <u>When</u> should you be baptized and <u>why</u>?

Acts 2:38-41

_____

_____

Acts 8:12-13

_____

_____

Acts 8:30-39

Acts 16:14-15

Acts 16:29-34

Acts 18:8

Acts 19:4-5

Developing a Spiritual Foundation

2. When should a person be baptized? (Choose your answer from the recent verses.)

_____

_____

3. In Lesson #1 ("My New Security in Christ"), you learned that you become a Christian... (how?)

_____ By living a good life.

_____ By doing religious things like going to church, reading Bible, and praying.

_____ By obeying strict commandments (laws) of God.

_____ By having personal faith in the Lord Jesus Christ and believe that He died on the cross for my sins.

_____ I am not sure, I don't know.

Important note: The Bible teaches that no one is saved through their own good works (Romans 4:1-8). You are not saved because you go to church and practice religious services (Romans 4:9-12). You are not saved because you obey righteous laws (Romans 4:13-14). You can be saved only through personal faith in God's Son, Jesus Christ, and His death on the cross that paid the punishment for your sins. (Romans 3:21-31, and Ephesians 2:8-9). The Bible explains that baptism is just a physical mark/image of what happened to you inside spiritually. Baptism is like a wedding ring—it's a mark/image in your heart that you make a promise & commitment (responsibility) in your heart towards Jesus.

5. Baptism is a mark/image of a reminder of our faith, promise, & responsibility to God.

a. How did Joshua remind God's people of their faith, promise, and responsibility to God? Read Joshua 24:17-28.

b. What image or example did Paul use to remind God's people of their faith, promise, and responsibility? Read Romans 6:1-4.

Developing a Spiritual Foundation

6. Baptism reminds us of our new... (what?)

a. Read Romans 6:3-5

_____

_____

b. Read Romans 6:4

_____

_____

7. Why should we want to be baptized?

a. Read Matthew 28:19-20

_____

b. Read Matthew 3:13-16

_____

42

8. Why should I be baptized by immersion and not sprinkle water on my head?

Note: You will see this word "immerse" or "immersion" often in this lesson. The words mean to "fully dip under the water" (100% of all your body & head down under water). The English word "baptize" is a transliteration of the Greek word "baptizo," and translated it means "to dip under" or to "immerse." You can look back to this note as a reminder.

a. Read Matthew 3:16. Because _____ was baptized that way.

b. Because the word "baptize" means

_____

_____

c. Immersion is the best way to show a clear picture of Jesus death, burial, and resurrection (to rise from the dead), as taught by church leaders/founders.

Martin Luther said, "I would have those who are to be baptized to be entirely immersed, (put under water), as the word imparts (instructs) and the mystery (puzzlement) signifies (shows/answers through action)."

John Calvin said, "The word 'baptize' signifies (means) to me to immerse. It is certain that immersion was the practice (way of doing) of the ancient (early/beginning) church."

John Wesley said, "Buried with Him, alluding (to refer) to baptizing by immersion according (relating) to the custom (routine) of the first church."

Important Note: Some churches practice a "baptism of conversion (spiritual change)" for children. This ceremony is seen as the removal of old/past sin and the giving of grace to the child. Some churches practice a "baptism of confirmation (approved acceptance)" for children. This formal service is seen as a promise/oath between the parents and God relating to their child. These customs began about 400 AD.

The baptism of the New Testament is a "baptism of confession (telling personal experience of faith)." The purpose is to openly tell others about your personal faith and promise to Christ. Baptism was very important to the believers in the beginning churches of long ago. There is only one time in history (in the book of Acts), where a new believer wasn't baptized on the same day he was saved. Read Acts 9:1-19.

9. What is a confession (telling personal truth) of faith?

_____

_____

10. Think carefully about this lesson. How do you feel?

_____ I feel confused.

_____ I feel frustrated.

_____ I understand about baptism.

_____ I feel it is a tough decision, and I will think about baptism.

_____ I want to be baptized to show my faith and commitment to Christ.

11. Explain why you feel this way?

_____

_____

_____

Weekly Assignments

1. Continue to read Mark (in the New Testament) and finish the book.

2. Next, read 1 John, 2 John, and 3 John.

3. Write your experience of how you were saved and share it with the leader, pastor, Bible teachers, or any other believer you are comfortable with.

4. Write down this verse and remember it deep in your mind. 1 John 5:13

Developing a Spiritual Foundation

Lesson #4

My New Family in Christ

Get involved with the church

Christian Life Quiz (Evaluate your beliefs before we begin Lesson #4.)

1. If I do not go to church

____ I cannot go to heaven.

____ I cannot participate in communion (Lord's Supper).

____ I do not obey God's Word.

____ I am not part of God's family.

2. "Why" should I go to church?

____ To receive forgiveness of sins

____ To receive salvation through the church

____ Believers will help encourage me.

____ To help the church fulfill God's mission

____ For accountability (God's people can help me be loyal & obedient to God's Word.)

Lesson #4: My New Family in Christ: Get involved with the church

1. Before you were saved, why did you go to church? What motivated you?

2. You should become a member of a church because this is God's will for you.

a. Read Hebrews 10:25. Write down the sentence (from this verse) that says we should go to church regularly (every week).

b. Read Hebrews 10:24-25. What good things do you get for going to church?

Developing a Spiritual Foundation

c. Read Hebrews 10:24-25. When you go to church; what should your attitude be?

_____

_____

3. The first Christians (in the Bible) were faithful to… (what?)

Read Acts 2:42-47 and write down answers.

a. They were faithful to

_____

b. They were faithful to

_____

c. They were faithful to

_____

d. They were faithful to

e. They were faithful to

f. They were faithful to

g. They were faithful to

4. There are good things you can get fellowshipping in big and small groups of Christians. Write down good things you can get from each group.

a. Good things from small groups

b. Good things from big groups

5. Read Psalm 133:1, and write down two positive (good) reasons why you need to belong to God's family.

a. It is

b. It is

6. In Psalm 133:1, as "brethren" (brothers & sisters in Christ) together (all of us), we are... (what?)

a. Ephesians 4:3 says, "Make every effort (do your best) to keep yourselves united (connected) in the Spirit..." Unity (all of us connected) involves active work. We cannot sit back and do nothing. We must be involved in each other's lives. Read Ephesians 4:2 and write down four attitudes we must have.

1.

2.

3.

4.

b. Read Ephesians 4:4-6. Write down the reason we should want to be in unity (all of us connected).

_____

_____

_____

c. Do you know someone (one person) in church that is hard to get along with (not friendly, hard feelings, angry, etc.)? Or a group of people (many people together) in church that is hard to get along with (not friendly, hard feelings, angry, etc.)? What should you do?

_____ avoid them in public

_____ criticize them privately

_____ talk to them carefully <u>with love and respect</u>

_____ judge them in my mind

_____ I don't know what to do.

Developing a Spiritual Foundation

d. The Bible explains ways we can remain in unity (stay connected). Read the following verses and explain what they mean.

Romans 12:3

Romans 12:10

Romans 12:13

Romans 12:16

Romans 13:8

55

Romans 14:1

Romans 14:13

Romans 14:19

Romans 15:7

Developing a Spiritual Foundation

e. If you are in unity with other believers, you are still same person. But God gives you special gifts that "fit/join" you together into one body of Christ. Read Romans 12:4-8 and 1 Corinthians 12:12-26 and then explain how you become one body of Christ…fitted (matched) perfectly together in unity (connection).

f. List 3 attitudes you should show toward other people (who are hard to get along with).

1.

2.

3.

g. Write down 3 steps to help you find unity (connection) and fellowship with another person.

1. _____

_____

2. _____

_____

3. _____

_____

7. Write down the things you learned in this lesson.

_____

_____

_____

_____

Weekly Assignments

1. Read the book of Ephesians.

2. Join a small group event/opportunity at church. (Try at least one time.)

3. This week find out how a person becomes a member of a church.

4. Write down and remember deep in your mind this verse: Romans 15:7

_____

_____

_____

_____

_____

5. Encourage someone this week and send them a note of appreciation. (Tell them you are thankful for them, or appreciate their kindness, etc.)

Developing a Spiritual Foundation

Lesson #5

My New Freedom in Christ

How to experience God's forgiveness

Christian Life Quiz

(Evaluate your beliefs before we begin Lesson #5.)

Put a check mark by the sentences that are true about you.

____ In past, I had bad relationship with my father/mother.

____ It is hard for me to believe God loves me.

____ It is hard to forgive myself when I did hurt other people.

____ I cannot forgive myself for my past sins.

____ I cannot forgive other people who hurt me bad.

____ Most of the time I worry and feel afraid about situations out of control.

____ I have sinful habits in my life I cannot break. (Can't stop sinning).

____ In the past, people with higher authority hurt me.

____ In the past, I was involved in occult things (like witchcraft, seances, etc.).

____ When I go to church, it is hard to concentrate/focus.

____ It is hard for me to focus reading the Bible and praying.

_____ I have addictions (like eating too much, gambling, smoking, drugs, alcohol, telling lies, gossiping, etc.).

_____ I have secret addictions I hide.

Lesson #5: My New Freedom in Christ: How to experience God's forgiveness

1. In Romans 3:20, we see the Bible's definition of guilt. What does guilt mean? Write your own words.

_____

_____

2. Read Luke 18:9-14 and answer these questions.

a. Can you be guilty, but you don't understand that you are guilty?

_____

_____

b. When you realize (notice/feel) you are guilty, what should you do?

_____

_____

Developing a Spiritual Foundation

c. In Luke 18:9-14, who was forgiven? Why was he forgiven?

d. Read 1 John 1:9. What should you do when you realize (notice/feel) you are guilty?

3. Read Isaiah 1:4-5. Why do you continue feeling guilty?

4. Read Psalm 38:1-14. Write down the consequences (result) when your heart refuses to repent.

a. Spiritual consequences (result)

b. Emotional consequences (result)

c. Relationship consequences (result)

d. Physical consequences (result)

5. If you don't admit your sins (say you don't sin), what does the Bible say about you?

a. 1 John 1:6

b. 1 John 1:8

c. 1 John 1:10

Something to think about

"[In the past,] the Indians [Native Americans] used to say that within [inside] every [person's] heart there is a knife. This knife turns like the minute hand on a clock. Every time the heart lies, the knife rotates an increment [turns a little bit]. As it turns, it cuts into the heart. As it turns, it carves [cuts out] a circle. The more it turns, the wider the circle becomes. After the knife has rotated one full circle, a path has been carved. The result? No more hurt, no more heart. [It is gone.]"

From "Finding a Father's Love," by Max Lucado

https://maxlucado.com/read/topical/finding-a-fathers-love/

6. Read Romans 3:22-26. Who can set you free from guilt and pain in your past? Explain how He did it.

What is my responsibility (duty) in the process?

7. Because of your faith in Christ, God says many wonderful things about you (speaking about you personally). Write down what those things are in your own words.

a. John 1:12

b. John 15:15

c. Romans 8:1

d. 1 Corinthians 6:19-20

e. 2 Corinthians 5:17

f. Ephesians 2:10

g. Colossians 1:14

h. 1 John 5:18

Developing a Spiritual Foundation

8. After you become a Christian, what should you do when you fall into sin again?

a. Psalm 32:5

b. James 5:16

9. After you confess your sins, you should also… (do what?)

a. Proverbs 28:13

Explain how to stop sinning.

b. Joel 2:12-13

What does repentance mean?

10. When you repent and confess your sin, God will respond to you in a positive way.

a. Psalm 103:10,12

b. Isaiah 43:25

11. Finish these sentences below and discuss them in class.

In this lesson, I learned

Developing a Spiritual Foundation

This lesson helped me believe

_____

_____

_____

I feel

_____

_____

_____

Write a short prayer to thank God for what you learned.

_____

_____

_____

_____

Developing a Spiritual Foundation

Weekly Assignments

1. Begin reading the book of John.

2. Get two 3x5 cards and write these Bible verses:

Isaiah 43:25. Write all the verse on one side of card. When you finish, then turn the card over and write this: "When I confess my sin, God will erase my sin and never think about my sin."

1 John 1:9. Write all the verse on one side of card. When you finish, then turn the card over and write this: "When I confess my sins, God is faithful to forgive me and make me clean."

3. Memorize (remember deep in your mind) 1 John 1:9.

4. Share one truth from this lesson with a friend.

Lesson #6

My New Road Map for Life

Understanding the Bible

Christian Life Quiz

(Evaluate your beliefs before we begin Lesson #6.)

I know some people think:

_____ The Bible is like fairy tale stories (imaginary/fiction/not real).

_____ The Bible is dangerous to read.

_____ The Bible is mythological (means imaginary/fiction/not real).

_____ The Bible is records of true history.

_____ The Bible is Word of God.

_____ The Bible was written after Jesus died on cross.

Developing a Spiritual Foundation

Write your opinion about the Bible. What does the Bible mean to you?

_____

_____

_____

_____

_____

Lesson #6: My New Road Map for Life: Understanding the Bible

The Bible is one book (with a collection of 66 books inside). It is very special, and there is no other book like it. How long did it take to write the Bible? More than 60 generations, over 1,600 years, and 40 different people wrote the books. Who were these authors (writers of the books)? Some were kings. Some were fishermen. Others were philosophers (wise people), ranchers (farmers), poets (song writers), statesmen (worked in government), military leaders (soldiers), and also a doctor. The Bible is the "world's best seller," and has survived all other books. It survived through many years of persecution, criticism, and abuse. Many people attack the Bible, neglect (ignore) it, and abuse it for selfish reasons. But millions and millions of people studied the Bible and loved it."

Developing a Spiritual Foundation

The Bible at a Glance

Old Testament (39 Books)

Books of the Law
- Genesis
- Exodus
- Leviticus
- Numbers
- Deuteronomy

Books of History & Government
- Joshua
- Judges
- Ruth
- 1 Samuel
- 2 Samuel
- 1 Kings
- 2 Kings
- 1 Chronicles
- 2 Chronicles
- Ezra
- Nehemiah
- Esther

Books of Poetry & Wisdom
- Job
- Psalms
- Proverbs
- Ecclesiastes
- Song of Solomon

Books of Major Prophets
- Isaiah
- Jeremiah
- Lamentations
- Ezekiel
- Daniel

Books of Minor Prophets
- Hosea
- Joel
- Amos
- Obadiah
- Jonah
- Micah
- Nahum
- Habakkuk
- Zephaniah
- Haggai
- Zechariah
- Malachi

New Testament (27 Books)

Gospels (Story of Jesus)
- Matthew
- Mark
- Luke
- John

The Early Church
- Acts (of the Apostles)

Paul's Epistles (Letters)
- Romans
- 1 Corinthians
- 2 Corinthians
- Galatians
- Ephesians
- Philippians
- Colossians
- 1 Thessalonians
- 2 Thessalonians
- 1 Timothy
- 2 Timothy
- Titus
- Philemon
- Hebrews

General Epistles (Letters)
- James
- 1 Peter
- 2 Peter
- 1 John
- 2 John
- 3 John
- Jude

Book of Prophecy
- Revelation

Developing a Spiritual Foundation

1. How does the Bible describe itself?

a. Psalm 12:6

b. Psalm 119:89

c. Psalm 119:160

d. Psalm 119:172

e. Isaiah 40:8

2. What kind of attitude (thoughts, action, and behavior) should you have toward God's Word?

a. Psalm 19:10-11

b. Psalm 119:23-24

c. Psalm 119:34

d. Psalm 119:113

e. Psalm 119:120

f. Psalm 119:161

Developing a Spiritual Foundation

3. Why should we fear/tremble (deeply respect/honor) God's Word?

a. Jeremiah 23:29

b. Hebrews 4:12

4. Why do you think we should enjoy and love God's Word?

a. Matthew 4:4

b. 1 Peter 2:2

Developing a Spiritual Foundation

5. Why do you think we should obey God's Word?

a. James 1:23-25

b. 1 John 2:1

6. Why do you think we should meditate on God's Word?

a. Romans 15:4

b. Philippians 4:8

_____

_____

c. Joshua 1:8

_____

_____

7. Which one is easier for you to do? (1 = easiest, 2 = easy, 3 = hard, 4 = hardest)

____ fear/tremble (deeply respect/honor) God's Word

____ love God's Word

____ obey God's Word

____ meditate on God's Word

Developing a Spiritual Foundation

8. Why is it important to understand the Bible? Read 2 Timothy 3:15-17.

9. God's Word is important to you. Write down 4 things you can do with the Bible.

10. Here is a "tip" (advice) that can help you understand how to study the Bible.

> **T—Think** seriously about the Bible verses.
>
> **R—Read** it constantly (daily), again and again.
>
> **U—Underline** important verses.
>
> **T—Tell** others about what you learned.
>
> **H—Honestly** apply/live out what you learned.

11. Finish these sentences below and discuss them in class.

In this lesson, I learned

_____

_____

_____

_____

Developing a Spiritual Foundation

This lesson helped me believe

I feel

Write a short prayer to thank God for what you learned.

Weekly Assignments

1. Continue reading the book of John.

2. Buy a spiral notebook and begin writing personal Bible study notes.

3. Write down Psalm 119:165 and remember it deep in your mind.

4. Go to church on Sunday and share with a friend or family what you learned.

Developing a Spiritual Foundation

Lesson #7

My New Ambition for Life

How to honor Jesus with my lifestyle

Bible Knowledge Quiz

Mix & match. (Match books of Bible with the #.)[1]

____ Jonah	#1 Which is the first book of the Bible?
____ Daniel	#2 Which is the last book of the Bible?
____ Matthew	#3 Which book is a letter written by Paul?
____ Ephesians	#4 Which book in O.T. is a minor book of Prophecy?
____ Joshua	#5 Which book in O.T. is a collection of wise sayings?
____ Revelation	#6 Which book is a general letter to Christians?
____ Proverbs	#7 Which book is the history of the Apostles?
____ Genesis	#8 Which O. T. book is a major book of Prophecy?
____ James	#9 Which book is Old Testament history?
____ Acts	#10 Which book is called Gospel (history of Jesus life & ministry)?

---

1   Hint: Look at the 66 books of the Bible ("The Bible at a Glance" chart), in Lesson #6.

Developing a Spiritual Foundation

Lesson #7: My New Ambition for Life: How to honor Jesus with my lifestyle

1. Honoring Jesus with my new heart.

a. What makes my heart new? Read Romans 5:5, Ezekiel 36:25-27.

_____

_____

_____

b. Why is the heart so important? Read Proverbs 4:23.

_____

_____

_____

c. How do I honor Jesus with my new heart?

Matthew 5:8

_____

_____

Colossians 3:1

_____

_____

Colossians 3:23

_____

_____

_____

2. Honoring Jesus with my new mind.

a. Read Romans 12:1-2 and answer these questions.

What is a renewed mind? ("Re" means again), ("renew" means to make new again).

_____

_____

_____

How do you get a new mind? (What should I do to get it?)

_____

_____

_____

What will a new mind do for me?

b. Read Philippians 2:6-8 and explain Jesus' attitude looked like.

c. Read verses and explain what should my attitude look like?

Philippians 2:2-4

Philippians 2:14-15

Developing a Spiritual Foundation

Philippians 3:7-8

Philippians 3:13

Philippians 4:4

d. Why is my attitude important? Explain few reasons why it is important:

3. Honoring Jesus with my eyes.

a. Why are my eyes so important? Read Matthew 6:22-23.

b. How can I honor Jesus with my eyes?

Psalm 101:2b-3

Mark 9:47

Hebrews 12:2

Developing a Spiritual Foundation

Read all of Matthew 6:22 "The lamp of the body is the eye..." This explains why people say our "eyes are like windows to the soul."

4. Honoring Jesus with my new spiritual "ears."

Although your physical ears are deaf or hard of hearing, your eyes are your ears. You "listen" to things you see. But, when you "pay attention" or "focus" on something, you become influenced by that object. God wants you to "listen to" Him. Be focused on Him. Be influenced by Him. Do not "listen/look" to the world. Do not be focused or influenced by the world.

a. Why is it important to have spiritual ears/eyes that listen to God?

Romans 10:17

Luke 11:28

b. Read Luke 10:38-42. What did Mary choose to do? Why was Mary's choice better than Martha's choice?

_____

_____

_____

5. Honoring Jesus with your new voice/ASL.

a. How do I honor Jesus with my words (signs)?

Mark 16:15

_____

_____

Proverbs 12:19

_____

_____

Proverbs 15:1

_____

_____

Proverbs 16:21 & 23

_____

_____

6. Honoring Jesus with my new hands (things I do with my hands).

a. How do we honor Jesus with the work of our hands? Read the verses below and match the correct answer.

____ 1 Thessalonians 4:11-12	#1 By being generous (giving)
____ 2 Thessalonians 3:12	#2 By being productive
____ James 2:17-19	#3 By being respectful
	#4 By working out, (living) my faith
____ 2 Corinthians 9:6-8	

7. Take time (no rush) to finish these sentences below and discuss them in class.

In this lesson, I learned

This lesson helped me believe

I feel

Weekly Assignments

1. Continue reading the book of John.

2. Choose one area of your life that you are struggling with. Decide how you will honor Jesus in that area (area means in every situation, anywhere, any time—for example: sins, attitude, speech, etc.).

3. Copy Galatians 2:20 below, and remember it deep in your mind.

_____

_____

_____

_____

_____

4. Share your personal testimony, (how you were saved), with a small group of people this week. (Can be in person, VP, meeting, online, etc.)

Group name:

1. _____

2. _____

3. _____

Name of person:

1. _____

2. _____

3. _____

Lesson #8

My New Power for Living

How to "tune in" to the Holy Spirit

Christian Life Quiz

I understand the Holy Spirit… (Write "x" on sentences you agree with.)

_____ The Holy Spirit is a "force" in the Universe (like in Star Wars movie).

_____ The Holy Spirit is the 3rd person in the Trinity. (3 in 1)

_____ The Holy Spirit lives inside every human person.

_____ The Holy Spirit convicts people about their sins (causes guilt feelings).

_____ The Holy Spirit prays for Christians and gives them strength.

_____ The Holy Spirit gives people the ability to read minds.

_____ The Holy Spirit is a real person and He has feelings.

_____ The Holy Spirit gives comfort to Christians and leads them.

Lesson #8: My New Power for Living: How to "tune in" to the Holy Spirit

(To "tune-in" is like making many gears to work together/'running smoothly'/shift gears together.) It is important to realize (understand) that you (as a new Christian) have a new power living inside of you. That power is the Holy Spirit, and He gives you the ability to live the Christian life successfully. He is called "the Comforter."

1. When the Holy Spirit enters you to live inside you, what is it like?

Read Ephesians 1:13-14.

2. What does it mean that the Holy Spirit lives inside? What happened to you when the Holy Spirit entered your life? Read and explain.

a. John 3:3

b. Romans 8:9

3. Why does God give the Holy Spirit to live inside our lives?

a. Galatians 4:6-7

b. Read John 1:12. How do you become a child of God (what you need to do)?

4. Every one who receives Christ by faith, will also receive God's Holy Spirit at the same time. God promised He would give you His Holy Spirit. Read His promise in John 16:7-8.

As a Believer, you can react/respond to the Holy Spirit in 3 ways. Write down the 3 ways you react/respond to the Holy Spirit.

a. 1 Thessalonians 5:19

b. Ephesians 4:30

c. Ephesians 5:18

Developing a Spiritual Foundation

5. Neglecting (or ignoring) the Holy Spirit, interrupts (blocks) God from working inside us. We quench (put out His fire or stop) the Holy Spirit's work. How? Read 1 Thessalonians 5:16-22 and write down how you can quench/stop the Holy Spirit working in your life.

_____

_____

_____

_____

6. To grieve God's Spirit means you cause Him pain (like wound in his heart). Read Ephesians 4:29-31 and write down different kinds of behavior that grieve the Holy Spirit.

_____

_____

_____

_____

7. What does a believer look like when he/she is grieving the Holy Spirit?

____ happy

____ fearful

____ guilty

____ defeated

____ confident

____ satisfied

____ depressed

____ frustrated

8. Explain your answers relating to # 7 and discuss in class.

Developing a Spiritual Foundation

9. Read Ephesians 5:18. What does it mean to be filled with the Holy Spirit?

10. What characteristics or fruits do you grow when you are controlled by God's Holy Spirit? Read Galatians 5:22-23.

1.

2.

3.

4.

5.

6.

7.

8.

9.

Developing a Spiritual Foundation

11. How can you be filled with the Holy Spirit?

a. You must have a desire to…(do what?)

Read Romans 8:5-8

b. You must confess all your sins. Read 1 John 1:9.

Explain what it means to confess your sins.

Developing a Spiritual Foundation

Read 1 John 1:6, 8, 10. Explain what happens if you do NOT confess your sins.

_____

_____

_____

_____

c. You must make wise choices every day. Write down what you should chose…

Galatians 5:13

_____

_____

Galatians 5:24-26

_____

_____

d. You must keep in step with (means agree and obey) the Holy Spirit. What does it involve? (What will you do?)

Read 1 Corinthians 6:19-20

Read Romans 15:13

12. Finish these sentences below and discuss them in class.

In this lesson, I learned

Developing a Spiritual Foundation

This lesson helped me believe

_____

_____

_____

I feel

_____

_____

_____

Write a short prayer to thank God for what you learned.

_____

_____

_____

_____

Weekly Assignments

1. Begin reading the book of Hebrews.

2. Write down and remember deep in your mind Ephesians 5:18.

_____

_____

_____

_____

_____

3. When you return to the class, (next time), tell your memory verse (Ephesians 5:18) to the class.

Lesson #9

My New Choice in Christ

Defeating temptation in your life

Christian Life Quiz

(Match verses with correct concept)

____ 1 John 5:13	#1 Let Christ live through me.
____ 2 Peter 3:18	#2 Receive God's cleansing inside every day.
____ Romans 15:7	#3 Find peace and stability (strength).
____ 1 John 1:9	#4 Feel sure about your salvation.
____ Psalm 119:165	#5 How to grow in Christ.
____ Galatians 2:20	#6 Loving other Christians.
____ Ephesians 5:18	#7 Be controlled by God's Holy Spirit.

Developing a Spiritual Foundation

Lesson #9: My New Choice in Christ: Defeating temptation in your life

1. How are temptation and sin different?

Temptation is:

_____

_____

Sin is:

_____

_____

2. The Bible says temptation comes from 3 things. Write them below.

a. Read James 1:13-15.

_____

b. Read 1 John 2:15-17.

_____

Developing a Spiritual Foundation

c. Read Genesis 3:1-7.

3. Read Genesis 3:1-7 again. Explain how the devil tempts us.

4. Write down principles (rules) that help us defeat temptation.

a. 1 Peter 5:8

b. Psalm 119:11

c. Matthew 26:41

d. Ephesians 5:18

e. 1 Corinthians 10:13

f. James 1:15

g. 1 Timothy 6:11

h. Hebrews 10:24-25

Developing a Spiritual Foundation

i. Romans 6:11-14

_____

Write down the 3 strongest areas of your spiritual life. (Your answers are personal.)

1. _____

2. _____

3. _____

Write down the 3 weakest areas of your spiritual life. (Your answers are personal.)

1. _____

2. _____

3. _____

Developing a Spiritual Foundation

5. Jesus was also tempted by Satan. Please answer the following questions about that.

a. Why was Jesus tempted? (Read Hebrews 4:15.)

_____

_____

_____

_____

b. What kind of temptations did Jesus experience? Read Hebrews 4:15.

_____

_____

c. What spiritual weapon did Jesus use to defeat His temptations from the devil? Read Luke 4:1-12.

_____

_____

_____

6. Read Genesis 39:6-20. This is the story of Joseph and how he defeated temptation.

a. Write down Joseph's temptation (what was his temptation?).

b. Joseph defeated his temptations because he practiced (obeyed/lived) Bible principles/rules. (Look back at # 4). **What principles/rules did Joseph follow?**

7. When we fall into sin, how should we respond? Read James 4:7-10, and write down ways you should respond when you fall into sin.

8. Even after we fall into sin, we can feel relief and comfort (not lose hope), because we know Jesus will do…(what?) Read 1 John 2:1-2. Write down what Jesus will do for us:

Developing a Spiritual Foundation

9. This question is private—between you and God. Only you do this section. Only you see your answers. Below is a list of problems that prevent our spiritual growth. Read through the list and pray for God to reveal (show you) your problem areas in your life. Confess them to God and ask Him to help you defeat these temptations in your life.

Arguing
Bad TV programs/movies
Over-eating
Worry
Gossip
Stealing/shop-lifting
Alcohol
Using drugs
Hate
Anger
Abuse others
Can't forgive
Critical attitude (negative comments)
Judgmental (accusing others of sin)
Pornography
Telling lies

Gamble
Too emotional/moody
Obsessive thinking
Fantasizing/dreaming (extreme/overdo dreams)
Low self-esteem (thinking less of yourself)
Perfectionism (must do everything perfect)
Boasting about "self" (too proud of yourself)
Self-righteous (own good deeds)
Selfish living habits
Never satisfied (always want more)
Not happy/depressed

Make list of other things that you need to confess and ask God to help you with:

_____

_____

_____

_____

10. Finish these sentences below and discuss them in class.

In this lesson, I learned

_____

_____

_____

_____

This lesson helped me believe

_____

_____

_____

I feel

_____

_____

_____

Developing a Spiritual Foundation

Write a short prayer to thank God for what you learned.

_____

_____

_____

_____

_____

Weekly Assignments

1. This week read the books of James and Jude.

2. Review (look back and remember) Lesson 5 about Forgiveness. Read your 3x5 cards (that you made from the *Weekly Assignments* in lesson 5…1 John 1:9…read both sides of cards).

3. Go to church on Sunday and share the sermon with a friend or family.

Lesson #10

My New Privilege

Sharing my faith/witnessing effectively

Christian Life Quiz

(Put a check mark by the sentence that is true about you.)

When I think about sharing my faith, I feel…

_____ not worthy, because of my past.

_____ secure (safe), because of the truths I learned in these lessons.

_____ fearful (nervous), because I don't know how people will think and respond to my sharing.

_____ scared, but also believe 100% that God will help me tell others about Him.

_____ excited, because I know what Jesus has done for me.

_____ not secure (not safe), because I don't know enough to witness.

Lesson #10: My New Privilege: Sharing my faith/witnessing effectively

1. What does God want for every person?

a. 1 Timothy 2:3-4

b. 2 Peter 3:9

2. Jesus had a ministry on earth for 3 years with his 12 disciples. He taught God's Word and did many miracles. What was the goal/purpose of his ministry?

a. Matthew 1:21

b. Luke 19:10

3. How did the apostle Paul show his passion (deepest love) for the gospel?

a. Romans 1:16

b. Romans 9:1-3

4. Look (again) at questions 1-3. Finish these statements (write) short main points:

God's desire for people is…(what?)

_____

_____

Jesus' ministry/purpose on earth was to (do what?)

_____

_____

Paul deeply loved his ministry because

_____

_____

Developing a Spiritual Foundation

5. Which one of those statements motivates (encourages) you to witness?

6. What kind of message do we share with people? Read Mark 16:15.

7. How did the Thessalonian people receive Paul's message?

Read 1 Thessalonians 1:6.

8. When a person becomes saved through our message (witness), what is happening in heaven at that moment? Read Luke 15:10.

9. Why is prayer so important when you witness to others?

a. Ephesians 6:19

b. Colossians 4:3

c. Colossians 4:4

10. Something to think about

The message (Good News/Gospel) that we share about Jesus is a positive message; therefore we should speak in a positive way. This will produce/result in a positive reaction/response on earth and in heaven. Why is this positive message so hard to share with people in our world? Take time to discuss this in class.

11. When we witness, why is it so important to be filled with God's Spirit FIRST?

a. 1 Corinthians 2:12-16

b. Acts 1:8

Developing a Spiritual Foundation

12. How did Peter find out that Jesus was the Messiah? Read John 1:35-42.

13. Read 1 Peter 3:13-16 and write down all the characteristics (traits) you need to witness effectively.

14. More to think about

Sometimes we tell people more than they want to hear. For example, we might expose their wicked deeds all at once, and they will respond in a negative way. It is like pouring alcohol on open wounds. They might run away from us and not want to think about gospel truths that reveal their wrong doings. What are some gentle ways we can approach them and still witness effectively? Take time to discuss this in class.

_____

_____

_____

15. Here are some tips to help you start witnessing and sharing your faith.

a. Think about 3 people you want to get saved and begin praying for them. Make a list of these 3 people, (on line #2 of the *Weekly Assignments*).

b. Set up a positive relationship with these 3 people.

c. Share your own personal testimony with these people (see lesson 3 for help).

d. When you witness, keep your focus on Jesus Christ, and do not let them pull you into another conversation.

Developing a Spiritual Foundation

e. Focus on the FACTS of God's Word. Do not talk about other opinions.

f. Invite your 3 friends to your church or to a group event with other Christians.

14. Write down a prayer to God about what you learned in this lesson.

(Example: You might write a prayer of thanksgiving to God for the things you learned in this lesson. You can also ask God to help you apply these things to your own life. Speak to Him from your heart).

Developing a Spiritual Foundation

Weekly Assignments

1. Read the books of 1 and 2 Peter.

2. Make your own "Prayer List" of people who you want (them) to become saved. Start praying for them and ask God to help you be a positive influence in their lives. List their names here:

1. _____

2. _____

3. _____

3. Write out Acts 1:8 below and remember it deep in your mind.

_____

_____

_____

_____

_____

4. Go to church on Sunday and bring a friend with you.

Developing a Spiritual Foundation

Where Do We Go From Here?

First, let's review (look back and remember)

1. Write down what is the difference between seekers and followers?

A seeker of spiritual truths is:

___

___

___

A follower of Christ is:

___

___

___

2. How do you become a Christian?

_____ By living a good life.

_____ By doing religious ceremonies (traditional services).

_____ By obeying strict rules/laws (such as the Ten Commandments).

_____ By having a personal faith and relationship in the Lord Jesus Christ.

_____ I don't know.

Explain your answer (the one you chose above) and find the Bible verses to support/prove your answer.

_____

_____

3. How can you know that you are 100% forgiven?

_____ Because your life has no problems.

_____ Because you obey and follow some religious ceremonies (traditional services).

_____ Because you feel like a Christian.

_____ Because you believe and depend on what Jesus did for you on the cross.

_____ Because you had a supernatural (impossible/miraculous event) experience.

_____ I don't know.

Explain your answer (the one you chose above) and find Bible verses to support/prove your answer.

_____

_____

4. What does maturing/growing in Christ mean to you?

(Grade/rank the sentences below in order of importance to you. #1 means most important, #2 means really really important, #3 means very important, #4 means important, #5 means a little important, #6 means not important, #7 means totally not important/means nothing).

_____ being active in a small church group (Bible study, fellowship hour, etc).

_____ developing/growing maturely in my personal devotional life (reading & studying my Bible).

_____ witnessing about Jesus Christ in an effective way.

_____ finding out how I can serve in the Church.

_____ going to Sunday worship services faithfully (all the times).

_____ gaining deeper understanding of Bible verses.

_____ learning to give generously (cheerfully/not grudgingly/not bitter or sad) financially (such as giving 1/10 of your income to the church, etc.).

5. Why must you be baptized?

_____ to receive (get) forgiveness of sins.

_____ so I can join a church and become a member.

_____ so I can show other people about my personal faith in Jesus Christ.

_____ so I can go to heaven when I die.

_____ I don't know.

6. Why should you be involved in a church near your home?

_____ to receive (get) forgiveness of sins.

_____ to be encouraged and have accountability (be responsible to someone for the way I live).

_____ to receive and experience salvation only in church.

_____ to focus my money and everything I own on fulfilling/ doing God's mission on earth.

_____ to obey God's Word (the Bible).

Explain your answer (the one you chose above) and find Bible verses to support/prove your answer.

_____

_____

7. Finish this sentence in your own words:

In my own opinion, the Bible is…(what?)

_____

_____

_____

8. I believe the Holy Spirit is… (what?)

_____ the Holy Spirit is a "force" (power) in the universe.

_____ the Holy Spirit is the third person of the Trinity (3 in 1).

_____ the Holy Spirit lives inside all people.

_____ the Holy Spirit convicts unbelievers of their sin.

_____ the Holy Spirit prays for us and strengthens Christians.

_____ the Holy Spirit lives only in the hearts of true Believers/Christians who follow Jesus.

_____ the Holy Spirit gives people the ability to read minds.

_____ the Holy Spirit is a person and He does have feelings.

_____ the Holy Spirit gives comfort and guidance/leads Christians every day.

Explain your answer (the one you chose above) and use Bible verses to support/prove your answer.

_____

_____

_____

_____

9. Match the Bible verses with the correct meanings:

____ 1 John 5:13	#1 Letting Christ live through me.
____ 2 Peter 3:18	#2 Receiving God's daily cleansing.
____ Romans 15:7	#3 Finding peace and stability/security (feel safe).
____ 1 John 1:9	#4 I can believe 100% about my salvation.
____ Psalm 119:165	#5 Keep remembering God's Word in my heart.
____ Galatians 2:20	#6 How to grow in Christ.
____ Ephesians 5:18	#7 Be controlled/filled by God's Holy Spirit.
____ Psalm 119:11	#8 Loving other Christians.

10. Now that I completed all 11 lessons, I... (what?)

_____ feel more secure (not doubting) about my relationship with God.

_____ am actively involved in a small group at church.

_____ feel life is precious and I'm doing my best to live it to the fullest.

_____ was baptized to show other people about my faith.

_____ feel more peaceful and secure in my life.

_____ serve in a ministry at my church (or in another ministry elsewhere).

_____ shared my testimony/witnessed with some people.

_____ find more pleasure/enjoyment in giving to the church and others (rather than getting for myself), such as tithing (1/10th), or serving, or sharing things I own).

_____ feel ready to teach someone about God's Word.

_____ am experiencing God's freedom in more areas (parts) of my life.

_____ obey and do what God's Word says about my personal life.

_____ would like to witness to other people and help them receive Jesus as Lord and Savior.

_____ feel more comfortable (not worrying about anything) while praying to God.

_____ know for sure (100%) that God has forgiven me.

_____ bought my own Bible and read it often.

_____ am stronger spiritually and can fight the temptations that come into my life.

_____ feel that God has touched me and given me His power to live boldly in Christ.

_____ brought a friend/family member to a church service/ church event.

_____ read other Christian materials (books, magazines, etc.) and Christian websites.

_____ practice memorizing (remember deep in my mind) Bible verses.

_____ get along better (no fighting or bitterness) with other people, including my family and friends.

11. So now, where do I go from here? (What to do?)

Option # 1: Teach these 11 lessons to someone else.

Option # 2: Bring another person with you to the next class (on these lessons).

Option # 3: Find another Bible study where you can attend—to help you grow more spiritually.

Option # 4: Set up your own Bible study and invite your friends and a teacher in your home.

Developing a Spiritual Foundation

About Grace Deaf Ministries

Grace Deaf Ministries is a unique and challenging ministry that is affiliated with Converge Great Lakes in Madison, Wisconsin. Their goal and mission is to communicate the Gospel of Jesus Christ, in sign-language, to the Deaf Culture throughout the world.

Casey Porter (himself Deaf), is Pastor of Grace Deaf Church in Schofield, Wisconsin. Worship services are held bi-weekly, at Bethany Church in Schofield, Wisconsin. On alternate weeks, the Deaf join the hearing congregation (of Bethany), where Carol Fourman-Foral interprets the song time and message for all Deaf attendees. This blend of cultures have harmonized together as one body since 2004; and have found equality and acceptance to be a blessing among all brothers and sisters-in-Christ.

Carol is Converge Great Lake's Missionary to the Deaf. During the week, she and Pastor Casey reach-out across the nation and unto the ends of the world, by steering through the fast lane of multi-media and the internet. Bible Study Vlogs are posted on at least 12 different Deaf Groups via Face-Book and also on YouTube. Through the miracle of technology, God's Word and plan of Salvation are being preached in over 21 countries around the world. Contacts through Skype, Face-Time, and Glide open a window of opportunity to fellowship with Believers both near and far away. Jesus said, "Go therefore and make disciples of all the nations…" (Matthew 28:19). Thanks to the internet, God has simplified that command and brought its potential into our homes/churches.

With the permission of Gary Rohrmayer, (the author of *Spiritual Journey Guide*), they are honored to be able to print this study guide in a language that will be an easy read for the Deaf culture. In addition to this workbook, there is a DVD that accompanies these lessons, which provides a deeper understanding of the written text via video-signed-language. These videos are also voice-interpreted for the hearing individual who wishes to participate in the panorama portion of these lessons. Our sincere thanks goes out to the Green Bay Community Church, in Green Bay Wisconsin, for all their generous cooperation in helping to make this incredibly huge project become a reality.

Jesus did not come to save ONLY the hearing population…but rather He came for ALL…and that includes the Deaf people throughout our planet. "How then shall they call on Him, in whom they have not believed? And how shall they believe in Him of whom they have not heard? And how shall they hear without a preacher?" May souls be saved and all glory and praise be given to our Lord and Savior, Jesus Christ.

Printed in Great Britain
by Amazon